Other Books by Vinnie Venturella

Leadership Riches: Discover the Gold Each Day

The Epitome: Leadership Lessons Inspired by Jesus

*Cupbearer to Master Builder: Leadership
Lessons Inspired by Nehemiah*

*Strong and Courageous: Leadership
Lessons Inspired by Joshua*

The Timeless Book on Leadership

Meaghan's Little Book of Wisdom

Sophia's Adventure

*I Didn't Write the Memo, I Just Read It.
Selected Poems, Musings
and Leadership Observations*

*True Leadership: Leadership Lessons
Inspired by the Apostle Paul*

*Character, Competence, and Commitment...
the Measure of a Leader*

Heartbreak Ridge

DOLLARS AND SENSE:
A FABLE OF PERSONAL FINANCE

VINNIE VENTURELLA

authorHOUSE

AuthorHouse™
1663 Liberty Drive
Bloomington, IN 47403
www.authorhouse.com
Phone: 833-262-8899

Published by AuthorHouse 05/10/2021

ISBN: 978-1-6655-2531-2 (sc)
ISBN: 978-1-6655-2530-5 (e)

Library of Congress Control Number: 2021909634

This book is dedicated to my Dad Frank. He is a master of the basics of personal finance and lived the lessons espoused within this book. His example should be emulated by all parents.

Acknowledgments

Kids' first example comes from their parents, good or bad. Parents are kids' first teachers and everything they do is seen, heard, and more often than not emulated. I take that seriously with raising my two daughters and hope I measure up in all things. My Dad, Frank W. Venturella, Sr. was a phenomenal example when it came to personal finance. He's old school, like a lot of people his age and lived by and touted "the basics."

From my perspective he stayed well within a budget, did not spend on frivolous things, did not use credit, and saved his money. Even now as he's nearing age 77, he is still the master of those foundational principles.

I want to thank Rex Freriks for his editing of this book and for his advice on the cover, the content, and the format. I am grateful for our friendship and lean on his advice.

Contents

Introduction

It was a great summer day. The sun was out, there wasn't a cloud in the sky, the birds were singing, and the temperature and humidity were perfect. Tony just got back from his morning run and turned on the business news channel to see how the market futures were doing.

"Up three quarters of a percent," he said to himself seeing it on the television. He thought the market would be either flat or slightly up today based on his assessment of national and international news. But things can change in a second. Everyone who invests knows that.

Isabelle had just woken up and had come downstairs to start her morning routine. She mumbled "Good morning" to her father, Tony.

"Good morning, baby doll, how did you sleep?" Tony responded.

"Fine." Isabelle responded. She got her tablet and made her way to the couch to watch her videos. "Dad, what's the Powerball?" She asked.

"The what?" her father asked not knowing if he heard her correctly.

"The Powerball. The news lady on the TV said the Powerball was over five hundred million dollars." Isabelle repeated herself.

Tony looked at the television seeing the very end of the story but knowing exactly what Isabelle meant. "The Powerball is a lottery that will pay the winner five hundred million dollars spread out over twenty years."

"Wow, wouldn't that be awesome if we won that?" Isabelle asked incredulously.

"It sure would." Her Dad responded.

"Do you and Mom play the lottery?" Isabelle wondered.

"From time to time, sure, everyone does." Tony replied.

"How much does it cost to play?" Isabelle asked.

"Two dollars per ticket. I normally just buy one and have the computer select my numbers for me. But other people buy a lot more than that and use numbers that mean something special to them, I guess." Tony answered thinking about what he and his family could do with the money if they in fact did win. He'd have to remind himself to get a ticket.

At that moment, Tony's wife Michelle entered the living room having just gotten out of bed.

"Momma, guess what!?" Isabelle shouted.

"I need my coffee. Why are you yelling?" Michelle countered groggily.

"The Powerball is five hundred million dollars. Did you buy a ticket yet?" Isabelle sounded excited.

"No, I haven't. I guess I need to remember to buy one today." Michelle replied dismissively.

Michelle made her way to the kitchen and Tony gave her a kiss, "Morning." He told her.

"Someone needs a shower." Michelle smirked.

"I just got back from my run." Tony commented, stating the obvious. "When is Danielle getting up?" He added.

"She should be up by now. Please go check." She smiled at Tony.

Tony went upstairs to get up his teenage daughter Danielle. He smiled inwardly knowing she gets up when she has work, school, or swim practice but if she doesn't have to be anywhere, she won't get up early. Just like any other teenager he thinks to himself. He gets to her bedroom, knocks on her door, hearing nothing, he walks in. "Danielle, it's time to get up." Tony says. He has to tell her about three or four more times before he wonders if she is alive.

"I'm up!" Danielle yells.

"No, you're not, you're still in bed. Now please get up and come downstairs." Tony says as he leaves her room to go get a shower.

"Is Daddy off today?" Isabelle asks her Mom.

"Yes, he took today off." Her Mom replied sitting down to drink her coffee and watch the local news.

Danielle slogs down the stairs to the living room obviously not wanting to be up at this time.

"Guess what Sissy?" Isabelle yells at her sister.

"What? Why are you yelling?" Danielle angrily responds.

"The Powerball is at five hundred million dollars. Can you believe that?" Isabelle reports proudly, not really understanding how much five hundred million dollars is.

"Wow, that's a lot." Danielle responds indifferently.

"What would you buy if you won that?" Isabelle asks.

"Anything I wanted." Danielle responds in a typical teenage way.

A few minutes later Tony comes out of the bedroom dressed casually, having just gotten a shower.

"Dad said he was going to buy a Powerball ticket today, didn't you?" Isabelle announced to the family.

"I didn't actually say I was going to buy one, but I guess I better, just in case." He smiles at his wife Michelle as he says it.

"Dad, would you stop working if we won the Powerball?" Danielle asked with a little more seriousness than normal.

"I'm sure I would. Most people do." Tony continued. "Let's not think about that right now. I work like most people because I must and happen to love my job and I get to help a lot of people while doing my job. But I guess like most people if money was not an issue, I would do what I really love to do." Tony finished, hoping to put an end to the Powerball conversation.

"So, you aren't doing what you really love to do?" Isabelle asked.

"I love my job, but no if I didn't "have to" (Tony used air quotes for emphasis) work where I work, I would do something else." Tony answered looking at Michelle but also thinking inside that he wished he could write full-time. Then he immediately chastised himself saying "hope is not a strategy," upset that the thought occurred to him. He continued the thought while fixing himself a cup of coffee that of all his books that he's self-published, they don't pay the bills so to speak. He has hope. "No" he told himself, he knows he'll earn traditional publication one of these days and then he can do what he really loves to do while providing for his family. Ever the pragmatist, Tony thinks about his current project that he's working on, does a quick estimate on when that will be ready for publication and more ideas race through his head about future projects. He's never at a loss for content ideas. He just needs to continue to work to get recognized by a traditional publisher.

"So, what are we doing today?" Michelle asks cheerfully, obviously done with her first cup of coffee.

Budgeting

"Can we go out for breakfast?" Isabelle asks hopefully.

"Sure, where do we want to go." Tony answers starving from his run.

"How about Cracker Barrel?" Danielle offers knowing everyone likes that place.

"When are we leaving?" Her Dad asks knowing he likes staying on a schedule and wants to maximize his time.

"We will leave as soon as I get ready." Michelle comments matter of factly.

"But what time?" Tony asks again.

"How does eight thirty sound?" Michelle states knowing she won't be held to that when it comes down to it.

"Okay, that's forty-five minutes, everyone go get ready, I'm starving." Tony reminds everyone.

Michelle, Danielle and Isabelle go to their respective rooms to get showered, dressed and ready to eat breakfast.

Tony goes to his office and was proud of himself that he had written one thousand words this morning for his current book before he went on his run. His goal is one thousand words a day, but he normally gets more when he doesn't have to work. He wishes he could write full time. He dismisses the thought and says to himself, "I am on a plan to get traditionally published and it's going to happen and going to happen soon." He knows he's set aside time later in the day to do some more writing. He sits down and checks his investment accounts, bank accounts, and gets ready to pay a few bills. Everything looks normal, as it should be, and he quickly pays the mortgage online and his water bill online. He assesses his budget and confirms they are good to go. He wonders about how many fifty-three-year-old married men with two daughters stick to a budget. He tells himself, somewhat cheekily, "only the smart ones."

Tony has used a budget ever since he got to his first Air Force assignment after basic training and the training pipeline for his job. It was somewhat crude. It was to simply get to the next paycheck before he ran out of money. He used a little ledger book because he liked how functional they were, always thinking he would become an Accountant. He first listed his income. There was only one, his small Air Force paycheck, then he listed his expenses and outflows. He thought back to those days and he initially got paid literally by check, then he had to go and deposit it in his bank account at the bank on base. He didn't have very many bills back then. He lived in the dormitory, didn't have a phone, and he paid what he thought was a small amount for cable television.

He really only bought food and entertained himself back then and had a meal card if he wanted to eat in the dining halls, where food was free. He ate out a lot which he quickly realized cut into his disposable income and fast. His budget was basically to have enough money to pay his bills, save a little and have enough to eat and entertain himself until his next paycheck.

He started reading books on personal finance and became more and more interested in the subject and the industry. He eventually hatched a plan in the late 1980s that he wanted to enter the Personal Finance industry once he retired from the Air Force. The first book he actually remembers reading was "Wealth Without Risk," by Charles Givens. He thought at the time there were tons of practical, common sense, personal finance nuggets that he liked, bought in to and has used ever since. He's been reading about personal finance ever since. He also realized that personal finance is not officially taught anywhere on a consistent basis to our youth or even to adults. He had a Civics class and was in Future Business Leaders of America in high school, but there was never a concerted effort systemically across the country. He realized, next to his Dad's guidance, he gained the vast majority of his knowledge through personal study and has made it his mission to teach his kids the basics of personal finance. Along the way he hopes they gain a passion for self-study as well. Things change so fast, but the basics will always remain the same and he feels if someone can master those, they can master their financial life.

"Let's go Dad. It's time to eat!" Isabelle yells from the bottom of the stairs seemingly at her Dad.

"Why are you yelling?" He asks puzzled that for once his family was waiting on him to go eat.

Tony, Michelle, Danielle and Isabelle loaded into Michelle's 2009 Acura MDX to go to breakfast. Michelle bought it used and loves it. She's always bought used cars and swears by it because of the savings. Because of how they build cars these days, most of them last forever if you take care of them.

"I like Cracker Barrel." Isabelle announced

Everyone smiled. They all liked Cracker Barrel.

"I think it's cool we can eat out whenever we want to." Danielle opines. "It seems like a lot of people only go out on special occasions or hardly at all." She finishes her statement.

"We eat out too much. When I was little, we NEVER ate out at all." Michelle announced proudly. Danielle and Isabelle gave that knowing look like "here we go again."

"I'm serious. We never had the money. We always ate at home. Momma would make us full course meals every night and we always ate them together as a family. We had lots of vegetables, rice, potatoes and chicken or beef. We never had the stuff you kids have today." Michelle seemed somewhat upset about it.

Tony interjected. "We eat out because I like to eat out. Your Mom and I have sacrificed and budgeted so we can enjoy the things we want and eating out is one of them. You guys know I cook a lot at home and make good meals for the whole family. I love to cook, but I also love to eat out."

"What's a budget?" Isabelle asked as they pulled into the Cracker Barrell parking lot.

"It's basically spending only what you can afford to." Tony replied.

Michelle parked the car and they walked to the hostess and signed up for the wait. The waitress said it would only be about fifteen minutes. Michelle decided to look around the country store for stuff everyone knew she didn't need.

Tony found a corner out of the way of everyone near the hostess booth to wait for their name to be called.

Isabelle and Danielle went with their mother – future professional shoppers.

The hostess called their name and they gathered

as a family and went to their seats. They knew the drill, didn't need to look at the menus but did anyway, ordered their drinks, then watched as Isabelle played the golf tee, triangle game – whatever that is.

Their waitress came back with their drinks a few minutes later and then took their order.

"So, you can buy anything you want to?" Isabelle asked.

"What do you mean?" Michelle responded.

"Dad said a budget is spending only what you can afford." Isabelle continued.

"A budget is something I started over thirty years ago and basically makes sure we don't overspend, and money goes to where we want it to go not where we don't want it to go. Understand? The budget tells us what we have as far as income, from what we get paid from work. Your Mom and I then agreed to what we should pay for things, what we want to buy, and how much we should save or invest. A long time ago we figured out what we needed to have, like our house payment, insurance, gas for the vehicles, food, of course our television, internet, and cell phones, and our power and water bills. We also tithe." Tony barely finished.

"What is a tithe?" Isabelle wanted to know.

"It's giving ten percent of your income to the church." Michelle explained. It's being obedient to God, since everything comes from Him, He asks for the first ten percent of it back to help spread His kingdom on earth. Your Dad and I have not always tithed but we started a while ago and are obedient, but more than that we want to tithe. It goes through our church and they ensure it gets to the right places of need." Michelle finished.

"That seems like a lot of money." Danielle pronounced.

"It seems like it initially but now we don't even notice it. That's another reason we budget. Once you get everything squared away it's easy to stay on track. So, we've mapped out a plan, a road ahead so to speak. We spend a certain amount on what we must have, like I said earlier. We tithe, we save, we invest, and then the rest is to use for the non-necessities or things we want versus what we truly need. I'll tell you guys later about how we decide how much to save and spend each paycheck." Tony finished.

"Look, I almost got it!" Isabelle boomed.

"You always, "almost" get it every time." Danielle counters with air quotes.

Isabelle got down to two tees remaining, not sure how anyone can get down to one. Her Mom smiled and offered her some encouragement. "Nice job Isabelle."

Their waitress returned with their food, which seemed like a lot. They situated all the plates, condensed some, and then everyone grabbed hands in a circle (without instruction) and Michelle offered a prayer of thanks. Then they started to eat.

Out of the blue, "Dad what did you say the other day about 'the way to lose weight is through a caloric deficit.' What does that really mean?" Danielle wanted to know.

"Don't confuse things. There is a lot of opinion and noise on TV and the internet and I choose to ignore most of it because I know what works for me. The most important factor when it comes to losing weight or maintaining a healthy weight, is simple math. To lose weight you must burn more than you take in.

"For example, look at this breakfast. It's pretty big. To burn all these calories would require maybe one to two hours of intense working out. The key to remember is a cumulative daily count. All humans burn a certain number of calories just by being alive. The amount is based on your gender, genetics, activity levels, hormones, age, and overall health. So, if you got up in the morning and then just sat on the couch all day and did nothing but watch TV, you would burn calories. But what do most people do? They eat, probably all day. The key to losing weight is to have a net caloric deficit at the end of each day, every day for as long as it takes to lose the amount of weight you want to lose.

"This is done in two major ways, and I'll explain how this is comparable to our budget conversation earlier. The first way to get to a net caloric deficit is eat less. The second way is to burn more. And obviously combining both has extra impact. Now I am not talking draconian methods or crazy crash diet stuff here. I am only talking about making some minor tweaks. I work out every day. Some days are more intense than others, but every day. I know how many calories I roughly burn in a normal day just being alive. So, I strive to tighten up what I eat each meal and each day. You can even cut out a meal or two. You won't starve.

"The general rule of thumb to lose one pound of body weight requires the burning of three thousand five hundred calories. Most people can't or won't work out that long or intensely to literally burn that many calories. So, their choices include obviously working out but also eating less. So, let's do a little math. If you must burn three thousand five hundred calories to lose one pound, and you can lose five hundred calories per day on a net basis, how many days would it take you to lose one pound?" Tony finished.

"Seven days!" Isabelle shouted, smiling she got the answer first.

"That's right munchkin. Five hundred net calories lost per day, over seven days, equals losing three thousand five hundred calories over that week." Tony brought the lesson home.

"So, to keep things simple, which you all know is how I like it, (Michelle rolled her eyes at that moment) that could be a daily goal, have a net loss of five hundred calories a day, and you can roughly lose one pound a week, which most experts agree is an appropriate amount." Tony completed the thought forgetting he was at a family breakfast and wasn't supposed to be in teaching mode.

"Sorry I asked." Danielle smirked.

"But what's all that got to do with our budget?" Isabelle wanted to know.

Tony jumped back into instruction mode, "You can consider your budget like how much you weigh so to speak. You have two choices to impact your budget; generate more income, reduce your outflow or both. Let's say we are on a fixed income. Meaning we only get a certain amount of money each month and it does not fluctuate, up or down, month to month. To impact your budget, you must adjust your outflows. What you want your budget to do is be a slight net positive or even, but it's virtually impossible to budget to the penny. So, what we do is we know how much we will need to spend on the mortgage, on our power bill, water bill, cell phones, internet, TV, insurance, gas, etcetera. Then we know how much we want to tithe which is ten percent of our income. I simply give online every Sunday. There are alternatives, but that's just how I do it. I basically divide all of our annual income total by fifty-two and that's how much we give every Sunday. We also determine how much we give toward savings and investments. What's left goes toward those non-recurring items and normally our "wants" (Tony used air quotes again)." Tony finished while also finishing his eggs and bacon.

Michelle joined in while drinking her coffee. "I heard a rule of thumb for budgeting is the 50/30/20 rule. You allocate 50% of your income toward needs, 30% toward wants, and 20% toward savings. Have you ever heard of that?" She looks at her husband.

"I have, and it's a good rule of thumb. However, no single budget will work for all families. That's why you must figure out what works for you. For example, if you have debt to pay off, does that go in the needs, wants, or savings portion of your budget? Tony asked.

"I would think it goes in the needs section,

because you have to pay off the debt, right?" Michelle offered.

"I tend to agree, but I would argue to not have any debt ever, except for your mortgage." Tony said emphatically.

"No one does that do they?" Danielle asked innocently.

"There are lots of people that do it. I work with a bunch of them. Regardless how much money you make or how much net worth you have, you can avoid using credit cards if you simply live within your means." Tony replied.

"Mom said the 50/30/20 rule is a good rule of thumb. What do we do?" Isabelle asked curiously.

"We tithe 10%. I invest 15% in my work's 401k. I'll talk about that in more detail some other time. We save 5%. We allocate 40% for our needs. This includes everything we "must" pay not counting food. This includes all of our monthly bills: the mortgage, all insurance, gas, power, everything. And then we allocate 30% for our wants. Some of this can be saved, some of it covers those non-recurring, non-required items, and we also pay for our food out of that. Now it doesn't always work to the penny, but it is pretty solid and gives us some flexibility." Tony finished getting up to go pay the bill for breakfast.

They leave Cracker Barrell and get into their car for the drive home.

"So, what are we doing now?" Danielle asks.

"Who wants to go to the pool?" Michelle offers with a smile

"Last one in is a rotten egg." Isabelle says with a challenge.

Debt

On their way home from eating breakfast, Michelle decided to see how much her daughters remembered from their Dad's budget talk. "Who can tell me what the basics of a budget are?" She asked.

"It's spending less than you make!" Isabelle shouted.

"That's a great answer, but why are you yelling?" Tony beamed.

"It's a plan of allocating your income across needs, wants, and savings with enough flexibility, so that your outflows never exceed your inflows." Danielle answered somewhat professionally.

"That's excellent, girl!" Michelle responded.

They pulled into the driveway and Isabelle bolted out of the car to go get her swimsuit on and get her pool gear ready. Everyone else went into the house and did the same thing but didn't think it was a race. They were mistaken, Isabelle realized.

Isabelle got to the kitchen first, dressed in her suit, goggles on her forehead, pool bag with towels over her shoulder and grabbed the pool key out of a drawer in the kitchen. Michelle came in and asked if she had sunscreen, which Isabelle did. Michelle then went down the list of ensuring they had enough towels, water, snacks, sunglasses, etcetera. The girls checked off Mom's list. They got back in the car and drove the short distance to the pool. Isabelle had the key and unlocked the gate for everyone then ran to the spot her family normally occupied at the community pool. She dumped all her possessions on the lounge chair and jumped in the pool.

"I win." She shouts.

"Win what?" Danielle asked confused.

"Remember I said at Cracker Barrel, last one in is a rotten egg?" Isabelle said while masterfully treading water.

"Great job Isabelle." Michelle said encouragingly.

Michelle and Tony situate their stuff on the lounge chairs and go to the stairs that lead into the pool. Tony gets in the water and Michelle sits down on the stairs with the water barely up to her knees.

"I have friends whose parents already gave them credit cards. Shouldn't I have one?" Danielle inquires out of the blue.

"You live at home with us, most of your bills are paid by us, and what you earn from being a lifeguard covers all of your needs and wants. A credit card will only get you in trouble." Michelle answers for her and her husband.

"But they say they pay it off every month." Danielle offered.

"In my experience there are people that actually do that. They may have rewards cards where they get a certain number of points for every dollar they spend, and they can use those points for merchandise, travel or discounts. The concept is good, assuming they pay off the credit card each month. But from experience a lot of them don't. They start out with great intentions and then it becomes easier and easier to let the balance build up because it's almost insidious. They don't realize they're doing it. A few bucks here and there and before you know it you have a real balance. Then some folks will justify carrying the balance because the minimum payment is so low. This is a trap. Never, never, never only pay the minimum if you in fact have a balance on a credit card. This is a reason for staying on a budget because you will only spend money that you have already allocated. If you don't have it allocated, you probably don't need it. But if you need it you should save for it." Tony finishes realizing he was teaching again and not enjoying the pool.

"But what about emergencies? Don't you and Mom have credit cards?" Danielle thinks she has them now.

"Yes, we do. But we're disciplined with them, pay them off every month and what we buy is what has already been allocated for in our budget. We admit that when we were young, we didn't have a good handle on using credit cards but luckily got the message a long time ago. Many people don't and we want to make sure you don't unnecessarily build bad habits." Michelle answered in a motherly fashion.

"Some of my friends have balances on multiple

credit cards How can they ever get those paid off?" Danielle asks somewhat concerned for her friends.

"That's probably the most often asked question when it comes to personal finance and shows a lot of people's priorities are reversed. My goal was to never have any debt outside of a mortgage. But not everyone believes that. So how do you get out of debt? The first key is stop spending money using credit cards. Then pay off the one with the smallest balance first." Tony is about to continue the thought.

"I heard you're supposed to pay off the credit card with the highest interest rate." Danielle offers.

"That is still the widely accepted conventional wisdom, but again from experience there is a better way. Let's say you have four credit cards and you can barely pay the minimum on all four. Pay off the one with the lowest balance as fast as you can even if you must sacrifice in other areas. And pay the minimum on the other three. Once the first one is paid off, guess what? You have twenty-five percent less credit cards. Psychologically that will be pretty powerful. Then you take the money you were devoting to that first card and attack the next lowest balance with its minimum plus what you used for the first card and get it paid off as fast as you can, again sacrificing in other areas if necessary. Once that's paid off, you've reduced your number by fifty percent, get the picture?

"Continue adding the money you used for the first and second credit cards and add that to the minimum of the third (the one remaining with the lowest balance) and again attack it. Once it's paid off, do the same thing to the last one by using all the money you used for the other three added to what you were putting on it to begin with.

"Again, don't take on debt except for a mortgage. If you do, pay it off every month. If you carry balances your priorities are reversed. To pay them off, pay off the one with the lowest balance first and continue paying off each one (lowest balance one next) until they're all paid off." Tony finished hoping Danielle got it.

"Then guess where you're at then?" Michelle wants to ensure Danielle got it.

"I'm out of debt and I have more money to save, invest and do what I want to do, while not using credit cards." Danielle hoped she was right.

"That's my girl." Tony confirmed she got it.

"What's a mortgage?" Isabelle yells from the pool.

"It's a loan on our house." Tony answers somewhat methodically.

"How does it work?" Isabelle wanted to understand.

"The first things you do are find a house that you can afford and that you like." Michelle starts.

"How do you know how much you can afford?" Isabelle asks a great question.

"There are a lot of rules of thumb out there, but the first is it has to fit into your budget. That's why you should have a budget from today through the rest of your life. But the first rule of thumb if you're buying a home is the mortgage should be no more than 2 to 2.5 times your annual gross salary. So, let's say you make $60,000 a year. Your mortgage shouldn't exceed $120,000 to $150,000 total. The more you make, the more you can afford assuming you stay on your budget. The next two rules of thumb are kind of driven by the lender. Each company may have slightly different rules, but they generally follow these two. A person or family should spend no more than 28% of total gross income on total housing expenses. That includes the mortgage principal, mortgage interest, property taxes, homeowner's insurance, the utility bills and any HOA fees.

"The second is a person or family should not spend more than 36% of total gross income on total debt repayment. Total debt includes your mortgage, student loans, credit cards, car loans, etcetera. The reasons lending companies have these rules are to ensure the people have enough money to pay their debts. It doesn't always guarantee people will pay their loans off but generally speaking it's an effective way to put a limit on how much people can borrow to hopefully ensure someone's entire paycheck doesn't go toward debt." Michelle finishes getting a nod and smile from Tony.

"How come this stuff isn't taught in school?" Danielle asks.

"I am not sure, but I think it should be. Most young people don't learn this stuff early enough and some spend many years trying to fix bad mistakes instead living within their means early and often and enjoying the life they were supposed to enjoy. If you developed a budget that always stayed within your determined allocations for needs, wants and savings, no matter how much money you made, then you will NEVER get into financial trouble and your money can go toward positive things instead of paying off debt.

"That's another reason we use percentages because it's assumed as you get older, more experienced, more education and other factors your annual income will increase, but by sticking with percentages your wants, needs and savings are all able to be increased proportionally." Tony finishes.

"You make it sound so simple." Danielle realizes.

"It is if you develop a solid but flexible plan, stay discipled and committed to it, and adjust it along the way." Michelle offers.

"It seems like it can be simple if you don't want anything and live on the bare minimums but I like nice stuff." Danielle opined.

"That is a perfectly natural thought. But you must get this right. If you get this right, most everything else will fall into place. You have to stick within a budget, and it comes down to sacrifice. We can't all have everything we want. We may be able to get most things we want but we must save our money and get them as we can afford them. Understand? Please trust me on this." Michelle finishes somewhat emotionally.

"If you want to avoid debt, why do you have a mortgage?" Isabelle asked an innocent question.

"Because houses are normally too expensive to pay for them in cash. But let me give you some things to remember. Interest rates on home loans are very low right now, although they may change. They are incredibly low. You can do different lengths including 10-, 15-, or 30-years mortgages. The longer they loan the more interest you'll pay over the life of the loan. But what your Mom and I do is pay extra principal every month on our mortgage to pay it down faster. This is another advantage of having no other debt besides your mortgage and living within a budget – you have extra cash to use on wants, needs, and savings. We will definitely have our mortgage paid off before we stop working." Tony responded.

"So, if I heard you okay, you think it's a good idea to have no debt except maybe a mortgage. If you have a mortgage you attempt to pay it off early. And even though you don't have credit card bills, for those that do they should do everything they can to pay off the one with the lowest balance first and each one after that as fast as they can. But what about car loans?" Danielle summarized.

"We don't have car loans. We buy used cars. Remember, we paid cash for your car last year. I hate to keep saying it, but if you live on a budget and save for big purchases the way you're supposed to, you can afford a good, but inexpensive used car from time to time." Michelle answered.

"How do you save for big purchases?" Isabelle asked.

"We'll talk about that later. Let's get ready to get out of here, I think we all got enough sun for the day." Tony realized.

"Last one to the car is a rotten egg." Isabelle challenges the family.

They pack up their things and make their way to the car as Isabelle is there waiting on them beaming with her wet hair and swim goggles on her forehead.

They drive the short distance back to the house. As they enter the house Michelle does her normal Mom thing, "Hang the towels and swimsuits on the porch railing, put the snacks away and make sure all of your wet stuff is hung to make sure it dries."

Isabelle is the first one in her lounge clothes, things put away, towels hung and ready for the next thing. "What's next?" She asks.

Emergency Fund / Savings / Inflation

"Let's watch a movie." Danielle pronounces.

"Let's watch something we all like." Tony adds on.

"No kidding." Michelle smiles at her husband.

Danielle and Isabelle go to their movie streaming service and look for a movie they think everyone will like.

"I can't wait to go on our vacation next month." Isabelle announces. "Didn't you mention you would talk about how you save for big purchases, Dad? Isn't our vacation kind of like that?" She finishes.

"It is." Michelle answers for Tony. "Big purchases are considered those things you need or want but can't pay for them from your paycheck per se. You basically must save money each paycheck to get to the amount you need. These items could include our vacation." Michelle smiles at Isabelle for knowing a vacation was a big purchase, who promptly returns her smile. "It can be a car, a piece of furniture, something big for the house or even a down payment for a new house. It can basically be anything that costs more money than you can afford out of your normal paycheck." Michelle finishes looking around the living room to ensure everyone understands.

"But let's talk about a reason for saving money that is so important before we talk about saving for a big purchase." Tony interrupts. "The first thing any person or family must ensure they have is an Emergency Fund." Tony starts the lesson only to be promptly interrupted.

"What's an Emergency Fund?" Isabelle couldn't wait to ask.

"An Emergency Fund is three to six months of living expenses saved in an account to ensure someone can handle virtually any unplanned financial emergency. It's also there in case Mom or Dad loses their job, then we can lean on that until we find other jobs. Remember, I have talked with you guys about not taking on any debt. A way to ensure you do that, is through an Emergency Fund.

Here's an example. Remember last year my truck unexpectedly broke down and I needed to get it fixed? I used the money from the Emergency Fund to pay for it." Tony said grabbing a drink of his water.

"How does it work?" Danielle asked still looking for a movie the whole family would enjoy.

"As part of our 5% that goes toward savings, we make sure we keep six months of living expenses in a savings account that can never be touched except for emergencies." Michelle continues the lesson. "This account needs to be very safe and accessible whenever you need it. You won't need all six months of the fund immediately, but it needs to be accessible when you do need it. So, it can't be in anything that is risky or can go down in value. Once you determine how much you need or want in the fund, then you don't have to put anymore in there. Here's how your Dad and I do it. A while back we determined what our average living expenses were for a month. Then we multiplied that by six. Then we put that amount of money into the Emergency Fund. Once we got to that amount, we then continued saving money, but for other things.

When Dad needed to pay for his truck repair, he took the money out of the Emergency Fund and then we replenished it with additional savings from our paychecks until we got back to the six-month total." Michelle finished.

"Why didn't you use your credit card?" Danielle couldn't stop asking about credit cards.

Tony decided to quiz Danielle on his philosophy on credit cards. "What would have been the scenario that I could have used the credit card to pay for my truck repairs?" Tony asked.

"Um, oh no, you told me that. Oh, wait a minute I got it. You could have used your credit card if you could have paid off the entire balance within the next month." Danielle answered, proud of herself.

"That's right! Great job." Michelle encouraged her.

"Because the amount of the repair was the amount it was, I needed to use money from the Emergency Fund. So instead of taking on any debt, we simply used a portion of our Emergency Fund. Then all we did was replenish the fund over the next couple of months. That is a reason your fund should be three to six months of living expenses.

You probably won't need all of that money right away, so you've built in some safety margin." Tony finishes.

"So, we stay on a budget no matter what, we never spend more than we make, we don't use credit cards, we have an Emergency Fund to cover financial emergencies, and we save money for things we want but can't afford right now? All that sounds boring." Isabelle offers.

"You are one hundred percent correct munchkin." Michelle jumps in. You summarized exactly what we've been talking about today. But here is another thing to consider. Your Dad and I can afford anything we want, "because" (she uses air quotes) we do all those things. We don't think it's boring at all to be smart about our financial well-being. It just takes some discipline to get on the right track and commitment to stay on it. But get this; then you can enjoy what you want to enjoy because you're not worried about making ends meet and trust me that is not boring." Michelle concludes.

"What about this one?" Danielle offers.

Everyone agrees and she's about to push play. Isabelle runs to the kitchen to microwave some popcorn and get some other snacks and drinks. When she runs back to the living room, Danielle pushes play.

"What about saving for big purchases Dad? You never finished that." Danielle reminds Tony.

"We talked about how you build your Emergency Fund. You need to know the goal you're shooting for, that keeps you focused. Once your Emergency Fund is good, then you move on to your next goal. Your Mom planned our summer vacation and she knew roughly how much it would cost a while ago and then we committed to saving that amount of money in a savings account to make sure we have the cash to enjoy our vacation without going into debt. So, any time you want something, you first determine how much it costs, then commit to how much money you can afford to put aside for that goal each paycheck, and that's it. It's most effective to have a goal that you're saving for." Tony responds.

"What if you want multiple things?" Danielle asks.

"Great question." Michelle continues. "Depending upon how much each of them costs, you can save for both at the same time. But if you can't afford all of them, you have to prioritize which is most important to you and save for that one first." Michelle finishes.

"So that's where this sacrifice you were talking about comes into play?" Danielle states.

"That's correct. You'll never be able to afford all the things you want. But if you get on and stay on a budget, you can afford a lot of the things you want. A lot of times, if you are disciplined about only buying things you can afford or after you've properly saved for them, you may not even notice that you don't miss that thing you originally wanted. You must get in the habit of being okay with delayed satisfaction." Tony answers.

"Delayed what?!" Isabelle wants to know.

"It's called delayed satisfaction. Too many people want everything, and they want it now. Life doesn't work that way. Delayed satisfaction is simply being disciplined about buying what is most important to you, once you can afford it. It may not be today, but it could be in the near future if you commit to saving for it." Michelle replies.

"And what else?" Tony tries to quiz his daughters.

"By never using credit cards." Danielle is getting used to the game.

"Where do you put this Emergency Fund? Is it in the house somewhere? I've never seen it." Isabelle asks.

"Our Emergency Fund is in our savings account at our bank. But as I said earlier, it can be anywhere that is safe, accessible, and won't go down in value. Examples include a savings account, a checking account, short term Certificates of Deposit or CDs, money market accounts and other instruments. The key is it needs to be readily available when it's needed and that kind of narrows down your options." Michelle finishes.

"Do you earn any money while it's just sitting there?" Danielle asks a brilliant question.

"We earn a little. But with interest rates at historical lows there are not very many options out there that satisfies the requirements of it being safe, accessible, and doesn't go down in value. So, your mother and I have decided having a safe, accessible, account that does not go down in value is better for us for our Emergency Fund than the alternatives. A long time ago people could earn way more money on savings accounts, CDs and money market accounts, but the market landscape is not like that anymore and I am not sure how long it will take to get back to where it's a good option to put your cash." Tony explains hoping his two daughters understand.

"I don't understand what you just said." Isabelle said confirming her Dad's thought.

"Back when your Dad and I were much younger and even before we were born, the interest rates that banks would pay people on their deposits in savings accounts, checking accounts, CDs and other options were so much higher than they are today. So, a lot of people who wanted to avoid all risk could put their money in a cash account and still earn a little over inflation. Even though people may not "make" money (Michelle uses air quotes again) on their cash deposits, they may still use those accounts because in a lot of them they are very safe and accessible and won't go down in value and that's worth more to some people than earning money on their money." Michelle responds.

"What's risk and inflation?" Danielle catches on quick.

"Risk, from a personal finance perspective, is if your money can go down in value and at what rate. For example, if you put money in an FDIC insured savings account (below the federal limit) it is guaranteed to be there all the time. So, if you put one thousand dollars in an account today, you'll get at least one thousand dollars back tomorrow, next week or next year, not counting what the interest rate is or what inflation is. We'll talk about inflation in a minute. Some financial vehicles have a lot more risk where you can lose your entire deposit and in some rare occasions more than your deposit. We'll also talk about those later. So, it comes down to how much risk you are willing to accept on this particular amount of money that will narrow down your options. For example, your Mom and I are willing to accept more risk on our retirement accounts because retirement is so far in the future." Tony looks around to make sure everyone is still with him.

Michelle jumps in to explain inflation to her kids. "Inflation is the general increase in prices over time. Over a long time, it averages around two to three percent a year in the United States, but has fluctuated a lot during certain periods of time. When you bought those sneakers last week, Danielle, what did you notice about them?" She looks to Danielle.

"That they're awesome." Danielle said as she looked at Isabelle and they both share a smile as sisters do.

"What else?" Tony asks

"They appeared to have gone up in price compared to when I looked at them last year." Danielle realizes.

"That's inflation." Michelle continues. "So why is this important? If inflation is the general increase in prices, over time your money actually loses value just by sitting there. Here's an example; if you deposit one hundred dollars in a savings account that's only earning one percent a year, and inflation that year is three percent at the end of the year, you'll have one hundred one dollars in your savings account but the spending power will actually be less than one hundred dollars." Michelle completes the lesson.

"Then why would anyone use a savings or checking account or CDs?" Danielle asks intuitively.

"Because for some people they've decided it's more important to keep those monies absolutely safe versus put any of it at risk. They have decided, as your Mom and I have, that for our Emergency Fund in this example, it must be in an absolutely safe, accessible account that does not go down in value, not counting inflation, because of what it's meant to do." Tony replies.

"(Massive laughter)," from the whole family as a funny part happened in the movie at just that moment. They continued to watch the movie.

Healthcare Insurance

The movie ended and Danielle switched back to regular TV. Her Dad grabbed the remote and switched it to a business channel. He noticed that it was right before the close of the stock market and the market was up about one percent. "Not a bad week." He thought. Even though he reminded himself that it's the long play. A commercial came on that showed two mature adults, probably married Tony thought, talking about their healthcare and how soon they would be starting Medicare. They were discussing the pros and cons of their current plan compared to Medicare.

"What's Medicare?" Isabelle asks.

"It's healthcare insurance for those Americans who are 65 and older." Tony answers.

"What kind of health insurance do you have? Isabelle continues.

"Tricare." Danielle beats him to the punch.

"That's right honey. Because I retired from the military one of my lifetime benefits is Tricare until I'm 65, then Tricare for Life once I'm 65. It's our health insurance that you kids will have for a while with us, but not forever." Tony adds on to Danielle's answer.

"That's why you have to have a good job, Danielle." Michelle says but a little loud for the conversation.

"Why are you shouting? I know I need to get a good job." Danielle retorts.

"Healthcare insurance is an extremely important aspect of personal finance. Most people have it from their employer. Those that don't have it from their employer or anywhere else must purchase it on the market. And some people, depending upon their income situation, will use Medicaid. But I'm here to tell you, it's been terrific having Tricare all these years since your Dad was in the Air Force and now that he is retired." Michelle answers, but this time more reserved.

"How does insurance work?" Isabelle asks.

"All insurance basically works the same. A

client buys a policy to protect them from some risk, in this case ones health, and pays a premium or a monthly fee to the company. The insurance company pools the risk of a lot of people who have the same or similar policies to spread out the risk to the insurance company and hopefully require low premiums from their clients. Then if the client or their family needs to go to the doctor or hospital, they pay a deductible and a cost share to the doctor or to the insurance company and the insurance company picks up the rest of the cost. Without healthcare insurance it would be virtually impossible to afford visits to the doctor or hospital." Tony finishes his lesson.

"Having healthcare insurance is so very important." Michelle offers. "I know of a lot of people, including some of my family, that had it hard financially because they didn't have very good or any insurance." Michelle finished.

"What does all this say about healthcare?" Tony again quizzes his daughters.

"You must have good healthcare insurance." Isabelle blurts out.

"That's a good answer sweetie." Tony smiles.

"Having worked in the personal finance industry for so long and having seen a lot of people have it rough because of healthcare, I would tell you one of the best things you can do, besides have good healthcare insurance, is to be really healthy. Think about it. If you never have to go to the hospital or doctor, your healthcare expenses wouldn't be a thing at all." Tony said while getting ready to continue.

"Except for the premiums you have to pay every month." Danielle remembers.

"That's actually a phenomenal point. And it's true for most everyone except those of us who have Tricare and some other insurances but not many, who don't have to pay a premium. We only pay our deductible and a cost share, not to exceed a modest annual limit. If we don't use any healthcare services, we don't get charged at all. Staying healthy should be a high priority no matter how good your insurance is. It's less expensive and your quality of life will be a lot better." Tony responds.

"Is that why you work out every day?" Danielle asks.

"It's not why I work out, but it is a benefit of

working out. I work out because I love it. It's a part of my lifestyle and is not only good for my physical health but also my mental, emotional and psychological health." Tony summarizes.

"Health is as much about taking proactive steps every day to ensure you stay healthy your whole life. Whether it's working out, eating right, staying flexible, staying mentally active and not taking any unnecessary risks." Michelle adds on. "But we also are affected by our genes and those things we are predisposed to." Michelle finishes.

"What's for dinner Dad?" Isabelle asks.

"Well, I thawed out some chicken. Let me go see what I can make with that." Tony says going to the kitchen.

College Funding

Tony decides to make some fried chicken cutlets along with a full-course meal. He starts his prep. Isabelle comes to the island in the kitchen and turns on her computer and starts watching videos. Danielle comes and sits next to Isabelle looking at her phone.

"Did you and Mom ever save for my college?" Danielle asks.

Unembarrassedly, Tony says, "No." Then continues. "I always knew that I would pay for your college through my normal savings and from my paycheck. I know there are some options parents and grandparents have for saving for their kids' and grandkids' college." Tony says.

"Like what?" Danielle asks.

"There are 529 College Savings Plans. A lot of states have their own state sponsored plan that you can invest in. The positives are you can invest in a variety of vehicles like mutual funds, which are not guaranteed, and the plan grows and you don't have to pay any taxes on the growth and don't have to pay taxes if you use it for authorized college expenses. For example, let's say a child was born today. How long until they enter college from today?" Tony decides to quiz Danielle.

"I guess in about eighteen years." She answers.

"That's right. So, the concept is you open a 529 for a newborn and you have eighteen years to invest in it before he or she starts college. A lot can happen in eighteen years and the philosophy is invest over that entire time and the child will have a lot of money to use for college. Remember, 529s are not guaranteed. So, the owner of the account, normally the parent or grandparent, accepts the risk of the investment choices. There is a good chance the account will go up in value over eighteen years, but there is no guarantee and what happens if right as the child is going to start college the market tanks? These are things people need to understand. Your Mom and I saved money outside of a traditional college savings account and again we knew we would pay for your college using that, supplemented out of our paychecks as well. We feel this gave us a lot more flexibility." Tony explains.

"Can't you use your IRA to pay for college." Danielle asks.

"You can, but there are strict rules for its use and what is the main reason for investing in an IRA?" Tony puts the question back on Danielle.

"For your retirement, right?" Danielle answers timidly.

"That's right. Now don't take this the wrong way and don't take it out of context. When given a choice of funding your retirement or funding a child's college and you can only adequately fund one or the other, you should always choose to fund your own retirement. If you can save for both adequately, great then do that. We'll talk about it later, but funding for retirement is critical. You don't get a do-over, and you need to maximize your time. But for college, I know I could afford it without using a traditional college savings plan." Tony explains.

"What other ways can someone save for college?" Isabelle wanted to be a part of the conversation.

"Another popular vehicle is the Coverdell Education Savings Account and it used to be called an education IRA. It works like a 529 and there are a lot of rules and stipulations, just like a 529. A big drawback is you can't put nearly as much money in a Coverdell as you can a 529. But both grow tax deferred and both can be used tax-free for authorized education expenses." Tony answers while preparing the chicken. "You can use U.S. savings bonds as well." Tony offers. "There are a handful of other options, but all should be researched online with advice from a tax professional or a CPA because they all have tax implications for the owners and for the student." Tony finishes.

"It sounds like you had paying for my college as a goal but did not use a traditional savings plan as a part of that goal, does that sound right?" Danielle wanted to know.

"Exactly." Michelle answers as she prepares the ingredients for a salad.

"Don't get us wrong. Saving for college is important. Like any savings goal, the earlier you start the more you can save over that time and may be able to devote a smaller amount per month if you started right when the child is born than if they are older. Here is a simple example. Let's say you can save $500 per month for your child's college and you can start the month they are born and save until they are 18. That's 216 months, saving $500 per month, is $108,000 in 18 years. That does not take into account any return, fees, taxes or inflation – just math. But if the child's parents wait until the child is 9, let's say, they would have to save $1,000 a month to have that same $108,000 in the next 9 years, of course not taking into account any return, fees, taxes or inflation. The key in my experience is the physical act of saving the money on a consistent basis. Whether it's for college, retirement, a vacation, a big-ticket item, anything, the key is committing to the savings goals and doing it. Once you commit to the goal, then you can determine the best vehicle to use for the goal and your particular situation." Tony offers.

"It seems like a lot of this stuff is related." Danielle opines. "Living on a budget appears to be the mechanism that makes all this work, along with being committed to each and every savings goal. And I noticed you have enough flexibility in your plan to stay on track and still deal with emergencies and unforeseen circumstances. You guys also seem sort of old-school in being okay with delayed satisfaction."

Tony and Michelle look at each other and smile, happy their oldest daughter appears to be getting it.

"Who wants cucumbers on their salad?" Michelle inquires.

What if You're Already Wealthy

"It's time to eat." Michelle pronounces.

Everyone comes to the kitchen island to fix their plates. Once seated at their seats, they on cue grab each other's hands and Michelle offers a prayer of thanksgiving.

"How's the chicken?" Tony wants to know.

"We literally just sat down." Michelle scolds him knowing he wants everyone to like his cooking.

"You make the best fried chicken Dad." Isabelle gives Tony the affirmation he needed.

"We've been talking about some basics of personal finance all day. It seems like it doesn't apply to people who are really rich." Danielle offers.

"It might seem that way, but a lot of what we've talked about applies to everyone." Michelle starts. "For example, wealthy people need to live within their means, and need to understand inflation, and should have good healthcare insurance and things like that. But you're right. If someone is wealthy, they probably don't worry about having to save for their child's college. They probably already have the money." Michelle finishes.

"I wish we were wealthy." Isabelle pronounces.

"Why?" Tony wants to explore this.

"Because we could buy anything we wanted." Isabelle states emphatically.

"Is that all?" Tony urges her to answer further.

"It seems like things would be easier and you wouldn't have to budget and sacrifice and deal with, what did you call it, delayed satisfaction." Isabelle answers somewhat maturely.

"Those are great points honey. It would be nice if we were wealthy but it's not like we don't get to enjoy the life we have. And besides, once we got our financial house in order, it kind of works on autopilot so it isn't that big of a deal to maintain. Sure, there are things we can't buy today and there are things we can't do today but your Dad and I never felt bad about not being truly wealthy." Michelle answers looking at her husband.

"I don't begrudge anyone for their wealth, in

fact I encourage it. What is the motivation for wanting wealth? Is it to be able to buy things? Is it for status? Is it to make others jealous? Or is it to help others less fortunate than you? Is it to do good in the world? Or is it to build a legacy for not only your family but others to enjoy for generations to come? That's pretty noble, right? Your Mom and I have had pretty traditional jobs our whole life. We work for someone or some company and earn our pay." Tony was about to continue when his daughter interrupted.

"I saw on social media that's NOT what you should do." Danielle said while overemphasizing the 'not.'

"You mean working for someone or some company for your pay?" Michelle asks to confirm.

"Yes." Danielle confirms.

"Don't get me wrong. If I could work for myself and provide the same or better lifestyle for my family than I do today I would." Tony has a moment of vulnerability. "It doesn't mean I am not trying with my books. Of course, I want a better lifestyle. Of course, I want to provide more for my family. And of course, our hope is you kids have it better than your Mom and I have. That's every parents' goal. But I don't look at it the way those people do making it seem it's bad to work for someone or some company to earn a living. Your Mom and I love what we do. We are valued for what we do. And people are benefitted by what we do. All of that is important to us and is honorable and I don't think it's wrong. I also don't think it's wrong to want to be wealthy. The key point as we see it, are you benefitting those around you and those less fortunate than you?" Tony finishes somewhat emotional.

"How do people become rich?" Isabelle wants to know.

"There are many ways. One is because they are born into a rich family. They may inherit it from someone. They may win the lottery. Or what your Dad and I appreciate are those folks that provide a product or service that people want to buy. That sounds simple so let me explain. The Walton's and Walmart. Bill Gates and Microsoft. Steve Jobs and Apple. Warren Buffet and Berkshire Hathaway. Elon Musk and Tesla. Sara Blakely and SPANX.

Mark Zuckerberg and Facebook. And Danielle's favorite - Kylie Jenner." Michelle answers.

"Okay, okay, you don't have to list all the rich people in America. I get it." Danielle admits.

"That's not the point." Michelle continues. "What do all of these folks have in common?" Michelle asks.

"They're lucky." Isabelle offers.

"Perhaps, but there are other common denominators." Michelle pushes for more of an answer.

"I guess they're all smart." Danielle concedes.

"That's right." Tony interjects. "And they are also the best at what they do. And they revolutionized the markets they are in. And they generated a demand for what they offer. And as I mentioned, they have a product or service people are willing to pay for – a lot of people." Tony finishes.

Looking at Danielle, Michelle says, "One of the reasons I harp on you getting your degree and getting the most out of college as you can is so you can become smarter, so that doors may be opened for you, so you can see where you may add value. Yes, you must have your bachelor's at a minimum.

And more importantly, education will open up so many doors for you, especially if it motivates you to find your way. Who says you can't become wealthy? Why can't you be the one that discovers the next big thing? Why can't you be the one that develops the next greatest gadget that everyone wants." Michelle finishes in a very encouraging tone.

"I just want to be a teacher." Danielle says.

"That is very noble. It's a harder job than most people think, but it is extremely important. I attribute so much to some of my former teachers and college professors. Here is something to consider if you haven't already done so, and I don't mean this in a bad way. It's more facing of reality. Generally speaking, teachers are not paid a lot of money for how much work they do and how important their work is to society. You do understand that, right?" Tony asks needing Danielle to understand and be okay with that.

"I do understand." Danielle answers resignedly.

"No teacher ever got "rich" on a teacher's salary." Michelle offers unnecessarily.

"But I want my summers off." Danielle states.

"That's fine. That's where the tradeoff comes

that we've been talking about all day. You may have to give up certain things to have other things. No one can put a price on having a whole summer off. As long as you understand what field you're entering and what that means financially. However, this is why we are so focused on the basics of personal finance because you can enjoy the life you want to enjoy, be a teacher and have your summers off by committing to and following these basics." Tony is in teacher mode again.

"So, no matter how much you make, you should understand and practice the good habits of personal finance?" Isabelle summarizes in a phenomenal way.

"You got it munchkin." Michelle answers. "Great chicken, honey." Michelle tells her husband.

"Finally." Tony states.

"We need to go for a walk." Michelle tells the family.

"What time do you want to leave?" Tony keen on keeping a schedule.

"When we're all ready." Michelle answers somewhat sarcastically.

"Like I said, what time?" Tony can't help himself.

Buying a Vehicle / Vehicle Insurance

"Let's go." Isabelle yells, while in the kitchen ready for their walk.

"Why are you yelling?" Danielle asks.

"Because I'm ready to go." Isabelle answers.

The whole family gathers in the kitchen and leaves the house as a group. Tony has his camel back, his GPS watch, and everything he needs for a full-blown workout session.

"We're just going for a walk, honey." Michelle looks at him quizzically.

"You never know." Tony answers from experience. "How far are we going?" Tony can't help himself.

"Can't we just go for a walk without knowing the time or the distance or the route?" Michelle asks knowing that's not what Tony wants to hear.

They start to walk toward the high school right

up the road. Tony starts his GPS and takes a sip of water from his camel back. "Looks like they just got a new car." Tony states the obvious as they walk past one of their neighbors with a brand-new vehicle in the driveway.

"When was the last time you bought a new vehicle Dad? Was it Carl?" Isabelle wants to know.

"Ol' Carl has been very good to me." Tony says thinking about the name Isabelle gave his truck. "I guess it's been about sixteen years ago, and I'm still driving it." Tony answers proudly.

"Why don't we buy new vehicles?" Danielle asks.

"Is your car a good car?" Michelle starts the lesson.

"It is." Danielle confirms.

"When we bought your car almost two years ago now, we wanted to buy a good one but a used one. Cars last a long time nowadays and as long as you do your research you can get a good deal on a good car that will last you a long time. It can't be a junker. It must be reliable and safe. But you don't need to spend a ton of money on a nice vehicle." Michelle finishes.

"And we paid cash for your vehicle. A lot of people who choose to finance a used car will spend a lot less than a new one. And the car insurance is less expensive as well. Your Mom and I knew what we wanted to spend for your vehicle, and we stayed within that budget despite dealerships trying to get your Mom to spend more. Keys include doing your research, know what you want to pay and stick to it, and be willing to walk away if the person or dealership are unwilling to meet your desires." Tony summarizes.

"What's car insurance?" Isabelle asks.

"It is required by law and protects you and others if there is an accident." Michelle begins to explain. "If we were driving down the road, and got hit by somebody else, normally the insurance company of the person at fault would help pay for any damages and doctor's bills if we had any. Our insurance would pay for anything we were at fault for or pay if the other insurance company couldn't or wouldn't pay. There are a lot of stipulations but that's basically how it works. The key is you must have the minimum required by law, but we take the advice of our insurance agent on how much coverage to carry on our three vehicles. There are a lot of insurance companies out there and just like anything else you need to do a lot of research on cost, customer service and overall coverage. Again, there may be tradeoffs you have to make. Your Dad has been with our insurance company for almost thirty years and they have been good for us although we don't have a lot of claims." Michelle explains.

"How much does our car insurance cost?" Isabelle wants to know.

"We pay a fair price." Tony responds. "Once you determine how much coverage you want to have to ensure you and your family are properly protected, the insurance agent will tell you how much that works out to on a monthly basis. The total amount is based on a number of things. It takes into account the make and model of vehicle. Older, safer vehicles are less expensive. It takes into account how much coverage you have. You never want to be in an accident and your policy does not cover all of the damage to you, another person or their property. The drivers' gender and age are taken into account. Males are more expensive than females generally speaking. It also takes into account how many policies you have with the company and you may get a discount based on how many things you have insured with them. We also have our homeowner's insurance with the same company. And they take into account any other discounts like safe driver, multi-vehicle, and as I said, multi-policy. And one other thing they take into account is how much your deductible is." Tony gets interrupted by Isabelle on cue.

"What is a deductible?" Isabelle asks.

Michelle answers. "If you get in an accident, before an insurance company will pay for your share of the damages, they require you pay a portion of that total, which is called a deductible. It can be high or low. The higher it is, the less money you'll pay in premiums. The lower it is, the opposite is true, the more money you'll pay in premiums. Your Dad and I have decided on a middle of the road deductible so to speak, although we have only had one claim in like the last twenty years or so." Michelle finishes.

"I know you paid cash for my vehicle. Did you save for it?" Danielle wants to know.

"We had the money in our savings and had a feeling we would be buying you a car eventually. But yes, for all big ticket purchases we follow our process of putting money aside each paycheck for it to make sure we can buy it for cash." Tony answers. "But that brings up another point. We have savings goals all the time throughout the year. But if we have extra money that is not budgeted toward a specific goal, we don't necessarily go blow it just because we're under budget. We will let our savings grow and either let it stay there or add it to our investments." Tony finished knowing it was coming.

"What are investments?" Isabelle asks on cue.

"We'll talk about them some other time." Michelle responds. "How far have we gone?" She asks her husband.

"I thought you didn't care about the time or distance?" He responded sarcastically. "We are almost at two miles." Having looked at his GPS.

"Let's head back." Michelle suggests.

Life Insurance

The family is walking home. When out of the blue Danielle asks an unexpected question. "How much life insurance do you have Dad?"

"Where did that come from?" Michelle answers with a question of her own.

"Earlier today we talked about healthcare insurance and just talked about car insurance, and I hear people talk about life insurance from time to time and was curious." Danielle replies.

"Do you know what life insurance is?" Michelle asks.

"If you have life insurance and you die, your family gets some money." Danielle answers.

"Good." Tony continues. "If you have a policy, the named beneficiary, which is normally a family member, gets the death benefit if the policy is in force when the insured person dies. Understand so far?" Tony is in teaching mode.

"Yep." Danielle offers.

"Generally speaking, people have life insurance on themselves, their spouse or children to help take care of the survivors once the insured dies. From experience, a lot of people don't have any life insurance or too little life insurance." Tony says somewhat emotionally.

"How much do you have?" Isabelle asks.

"I have a lot. What can I guarantee every single person on this planet will do?" Tony quizzes his daughters.

"Die." Danielle answers in an emotionless way.

"That's right. It's a hard subject to talk about for a lot of people but it's going to happen. We just don't know what?" Tony still quizzes.

"When they will die." Isabelle catches on.

"As Christians, our hope is everyone is saved, like we are. And as a financial professional, my hope is everyone has adequate life insurance. I know the value of life insurance and I know how bad it can be if a person doesn't have any or enough. So, when you consider buying life insurance you need to consider a few things. In no particular order, you need to know how much you need and want and for how long and what type of policy you need or want.

"So, let's say I want to pay for college for both of you (he looks at Danielle and Isabelle), and I want to pay off the mortgage, and I want to provide your Mom an income for life. There is a way to figure out how much that is. You then should determine if you want temporary insurance or insurance that literally lasts your whole life. Temporary insurance is known as Term Life Insurance and can be bought in various lengths of time like 5, 10, 15, 20 or 30 years. Term insurance is less expensive than the same sized permanent policy.

"There are a lot of life insurance policies that last your whole lifetime, sometimes referred to Perm or Permanent Life Policies, and you need the advice of a professional life insurance agent to talk through the pros and cons of each type of policy. For the most part, depending on the policy, as long as you pay your premiums, the insurance company will pay the beneficiary the death benefit minus any loans or fees upon the death of the insured. A lot of permanent policies are complex and have a lot of rules and stipulations and you must talk with a professional before making the decision to buy it.

"I've structured my life insurance plan to have both Term Life Insurance and Permanent Life Insurance. As kids age and mature, they no longer need to be financially supported as much as when they are children and live at home. And our mortgage will be paid off soon and I don't need to account for that forever." Tony looks to see if his daughters are following along.

The house comes into view as the family finishes up their walk.

"Let's finish this up once we get inside." Tony suggests.

Once inside everyone goes their separate way. Michelle into her bedroom to shower and get changed, Danielle does the same, and Isabelle gets on her laptop to watch her videos. Tony slips into some casual clothes knowing he and the family are down for the day. Tony goes to his office and gets settled to do some writing on his current book. Time passes and he doesn't realize how long he's been writing until he hears Isabelle from the bottom of the stairs.

"Dad, what movie do you want to watch?" Isabelle yells.

"Didn't we already watch a movie and why are you yelling?" Tony replies.

"Mom asked me to ask you what movie you want to watch." Isabelle provides context.

Tony walks downstairs and sees his wife and two daughters in the kitchen. "How about something we all like?" Tony says obliviously.

"Duh." Danielle answers for the family.

The family goes through the same routine as earlier, getting settled in the living room, getting snacks and drinks, finding a movie.

"Let's finish that life insurance conversation from earlier." Michelle reminds Tony.

"Why do you have a lot of life insurance, Dad?" Isabelle remembers part of the conversation.

"The biggest reason is I love my family." He looks softly at Michelle. Then he puts on his professor hat and continues. "Part of the basics of personal finance doesn't just include being on a budget, living within your means, being okay with delayed satisfaction, saving for things you want, not using credit cards and having an emergency fund, but it also includes being prepared for the worst things that can happen. No one knows when they are going to die, but we all will. I love my family and I truly understand the financial hardship a family will endure if the bread winner dies with no or little life insurance. That is not going to happen to my family. If I die unexpectedly or prematurely, it will be a bad day for this family, I'm being perfectly honest. Most families never have this conversation. And the last thing your Mom and you girls will have to worry about will be money. I've already taken care of that. If I die, your Mom is the beneficiary of some healthy life insurance policies.

"But we don't just have life insurance on me, we also have it on your Mom and both of you girls." Tony transitions into another aspect of life insurance.

"Why do you have it on us?" Danielle wants to know.

"A lot of people, and I mean a lot of people, do not agree on this concept. But let me explain why I got great, permanent life insurance policies on both of you shortly after you were born. But first, most people think that buying life insurance on kids is morbid or a parent's attempt to get rich when their kid dies or a scam by a life insurance agent. That is not accurate. Statistically speaking both of you are going to live decades and decades. And guess what you won't have to worry about? You won't have to worry about buying life insurance on yourselves. I've already taken care of that. Now as you get older and have a family of your own, you may want to supplement what your Mom and I have already put into place. There are a lot of people that, because of health or accidents or unforeseeable things, can't get life insurance. I don't think that will happen to you kids, but I've made sure that if it does, you will have life insurance the rest of your life.

"So, for the next many years, I will continue to own it and pay for it and eventually turn over ownership to each of you. From that point on you'll need to continue paying for the policy and you will probably change the beneficiaries to your own family." Tony finishes the lesson.

"Why does Dad have life insurance on you." Danielle looks at Michelle. "When he's the bread winner?"

"That's a great question. Just because your Dad

earns most of the money does not mean there won't be a financial hardship if I die before him. He will continue working of course, but there will be things that he'll have to do that I currently do for this family or pay someone to do if I am no longer here. It also will take care of your college and payoff the mortgage as well. Plus, it simply gives the two of us peace of mind knowing we have life insurance on each other." Michelle responds.

"Oh, how about that one?" Isabelle asks the family about the movie preview that's on the screen.

"Sounds good to me." Michelle reminds everyone who's in charge.

Danielle pushes play and the family starts watching the movie in relative quiet.

Investing Basics

The next morning Tony got up, grabbed a cup of coffee and watched a smattering of sports news and highlights and some regular news. After his first cup, he grabbed a second and then went to his office to do some writing on his current book project. He completed over one thousand words and was at a good stopping point. He then went and put on his workout gear, already laid out the night prior, smiling at how robotic he is at times. Today he was going to do "The Murph" with body armor.

Tony completed his workout and stayed outside in the garage to cool off while he continued drinking some water. Isabelle came to the garage, "I thought I heard you," she exclaims.

"Just completing my workout, baby doll." Tony responds. "What are you doing up so early on a Saturday?" He inquires.

"I guess it's the normal time I get up." Isabelle answers matter-of-factly and goes back inside.

He walked into the house from the garage, and Tony smiled knowing that Isabelle likes being on a schedule like him, and does better with a routine like him. He and Michelle have talked about keeping her on more of a routine schedule during the summer, on the weekend, or during a holiday break, since she thrives in that type of environment. But he muses, it takes the parents or at least one of the parents, Tony smiles to himself, to also be on a routine.

On cue, Michelle enters the kitchen, "Why are you up so early on a Saturday, Isabelle?"

Tony knows the answer is coming, "Because that's just when I get up every day." Isabelle robotically answers.

"I'm going to shower." Tony announces unnecessarily.

"What are we doing today?" Isabelle asks her standard question the first thing of every and any off day.

"I don't know yet, where's your sister?" Michelle asks.

"Duh, probably still in bed." Isabelle answers

wondering why her Mom always asks that exact question in the morning.

Michelle makes her way to Danielle's room and after tons of prodding gets Danielle up and out of bed. Isabelle can hear her angrily talking to their mother obviously not wanting to be up this 'early.' "Come downstairs and we'll have some breakfast." Michelle says walking down the stairs.

"Your sister needs to invest more quality time in her day than simply looking at her phone and computer all day." Michelle announces, overgeneralizing again but meaning well.

"What does invest mean?" Isabelle asks.

Both Tony and Danielle come into the kitchen, Tony from his bedroom downstairs and Danielle from her bedroom upstairs.

"Invest! Oh boy, let's talk about that." Tony pronounces, weirdly happy about it.

"Let's eat breakfast." Michelle commands in her motherly tone.

On cue, Tony grabs all the ingredients to make a big breakfast for the whole family and gets started on breakfast detail. Tony smiles at himself thinking of making a meal for his family as a 'detail.' You can take the man out of the military but can't take the military out of the man. Unfazed, Tony knows he'll make another masterful breakfast for everyone. "The term investing is sometimes confused a bit. It is simply committing something, normally money, toward an endeavor with the expectation of income and or profit." Tony starts. "See this breakfast sausage?" Holding it up for everyone to see. "This sausage is made by a large public company. If I feel this company is worth the risk, I may buy some of their stock. Stock is a share of ownership in the company. Small investors, which we and a bunch of people are classified like that, can buy stock but proportionally have little to say in the direction a company takes. However, each share is a vote and the more shares you have the more say you have. But for now, just understand that if we think this company is a good investment, we may buy shares of their stock. We would do that with the expectation of getting some form of income from them or the expectation the stock goes up in value." Tony looks around the kitchen island for understanding.

"So investing is buying something with the 'hope' it goes up?" Danielle asks using air quotes.

"Hope is a relative term." Tony continues. "Generally speaking, strong companies go up in value over time. They don't go up in value all the time and even good companies will decrease in value over time. A key is if in general the company is on the right path, it may make for a good investment." Tony finishes.

"Why would you put all your eggs in one basket?" Danielle asks ingeniously but not knowing why.

Tony brims with pride. "That's a phenomenal question. That is one of the rules of investing – do not put all your eggs in one basket. And we do not. We don't just own one stock. We own hundreds in the form of mutual funds and exchange traded funds or ETFs. Investing after all has risk associated with it, it's not something that can be completely eliminated, but the fact is investing involves risk. Investors take on risk for a commensurate amount of return. There are no guarantees with investing in stocks or bonds but all investors should be making educated decisions on why and where they invest." Tony finishes his lesson on investing and continues with making breakfast for his family.

More Than the Investing Basics

Tony was at work a few days later and his coworker John approached him.

"Hey Tony, have a sec?" John asked coming up to his desk.

"Absolutely! What's up?" Tony seems a little too amped.

John continues, "You know from time to time our organization is asked to deliver some continuing education or classes of a general nature at the local community college. Mostly adults near or in retirement take advantage of these offerings, but they're open to any and all students and they're free."

"I'm aware of those and I actually have taught some classes there and even attended a few as well." Tony sees where this is going.

"Good, so you would volunteer to teach if you were asked?" John implores.

"Sure, if it's a subject matter that's in my wheel house, absolutely." Tony's mind is already in overdrive thinking of what the subject might be.

"Everyone knows you're an expert on the basics of personal finance and the college approached our GM asking if we had anyone that could teach a class on the 'principles of investing.'" John uses air quotes, then continues. "That's what they mentioned to the boss man, but it's implied you can take this any route you think appropriate." John finishes.

Tony, with his mind already in outline-mode, says, "I got it. I will put something on paper and get with the college soon and iron out some details. Thanks for the opportunity, I appreciate it." Tony finishes.

After John leaves Tony's desk, Tony turns to his computer and says to himself, "the principles of investing." He mulls the road he wants to take in his mind and immediately types his four main points of investing principles on a blank document. They look like this:

1. Develop an Investment Plan Based on Goals
2. Create an Appropriately Balanced Portfolio

3. Keep Costs as Low as Possible
4. Be Disciplined Over the Long Term

Tony saves the document to his computer knowing he'll work on it at home later in the day.

After dinner later that day, Tony mentions to Michelle that he has some work to do and goes to his office. He pulls up the document from earlier and starts right in.

Develop an Investment Plan based on Goals

I am a huge proponent of having goals and plans for just about everything I do. Run a marathon in three months? I have a plan. Get my Master's degree in two years? I have a plan. Pay for my daughters' college education? I have a plan. Create a great anniversary dinner experience for my wife? I have a plan. You get the picture. Investing should be no different. You want to establish your investment goals and the plans to complete them. It can be rather simple and may be rather complex, but the principles are the same.

Your investment goals could include the following: retire in 2035, put a down payment on a home mortgage of $25,000 in two years, pay off a car loan in eighteen months, tithe every payday, or generate $100,000/year in pre-tax income by 2040. The list for everyone is literally endless. A necessary first step is truly ascertaining what you want to do by when and determining how much it will take.

An investment goal, like all goals, should be SMART. Meaning the goal should be specific, measurable, achievable, relevant, and time oriented. For example, "I want to retire in 2040, and have a portfolio that produces a pretax annual income of at least $60,000 that will never stop, as long as I live." That's a smart goal. Now you have to develop a plan to achieve that goal starting from today. And then you establish the goal and the plan for each of the things you want to accomplish.

Goal achievement should not be contingent upon extra-large investment yields, nor upon unreasonable accumulating or spending prerequisites. Delineating goals distinctly and being pragmatic about tactics to accomplish them can shield investors from normal blunders that disrupt their progress. Identifying constraints, for example risk tolerance, mental biases of the overall market and investing, discretionary monies available to invest, and time involved are all crucial when creating an investment plan. A simple plan will comprise SMART expectations about contribution amounts, contribution timing and time to monitor.

Unfavorable results often come from chasing disproportionate returns, the "hot" stock or mutual fund, investments or leaders who have unrealistic return expectations, or falling prey to the herd mentality. Chasing any or all of these are normal for those without a well-established plan and it even occurs to those with solid plans. More about the intangible long-term discipline later.

You must establish an appropriate plan with SMART goals in order to not fall prey to the whims of the market. You should never build a plan or portfolio based on temporary or fleeting factors. Those may include but not limited to the following: fund rankings, investments hawked on business channels, the social media mob, a get rich quick scheme, the latest fad or the latest technique. Any of these can tube your plan.

A solid investment strategy begins once you

determine your objective and any noteworthy constraints. Is it short term? Long term? Do you have multiple goals? How much capital can you devote to each goal? Can you put each goal on auto-pilot by investing in each on a monthly basis? Do you have to eliminate some debt to free up some capital? Are there any alternatives in lieu of capital that need to be explored toward goal achievement? What is the priority of each goal? What is your #1 goal? #2? And so on? Can you live without any or some goals? What level of investing risk are you comfortable with? What is the level of investing risk that you will absolutely avoid? There are innumerable questions to ask yourself and to answer. You must be open and honest with yourself and your partner to truly develop a solid yet flexible plan.

Clearly define each goal you want to achieve. Prioritize each goal. Develop a plan to fund each goal. Then stick to the plan.

Create an Appropriately Balanced Portfolio

It's easy to say, "just invest in the market over the long term and you'll be fine." That statement may be true for some people in some environments. All investing has some level of risk. Risk simply stated is the chance of permanent loss of principal. Some people do not want to deal with the volatility. Some are perfectly fine with it. I could argue that once you understand the long-term expectations of different asset classes, you'll become more comfortable with the level of risk you are willing to accept.

This is the first step...what level of risk are you willing to accept? Most every investment firm, individual advisor, academia, "experts," literature, and including but not limited to, private and public financial firms espouse using asset allocation to balance this risk versus reward. Conventional wisdom states the riskier your investments the more reward you expect and the converse is also true. Most place cash, bonds and stocks along this risk spectrum. One hundred percent stocks are perceived to be the most risky and one hundred percent cash to be the least risky (not taking into account inflation). Asset allocation is simply constructing an account with the appropriate balance of stocks, bonds and cash. Most investors would be well served using a basket of broadly diversified mutual funds or exchange traded funds to construct that balanced portfolio.

Some things to consider: the longer term the goal the more you "can afford" to invest in riskier investments and the shorter the term the goal the less you can afford to invest in riskier investments. All investing has some level of risk including but not limited to the potential loss of principal. For example, if retirement is 30 to 50 years away, I could argue you can't afford not to (double negative intentional) invest in a high percentage of stock funds. Conversely if you're saving for a down payment on a home with a timeline of say 12 months from now, you can't afford to be in the stock market.

I intentionally do not mention any specific companies (stocks or bonds) or any specific funds (mutual or exchange traded) or any specific firms (public or private) or any specific indexes or any named program. However, I implore you to spend just a little time conducting online research and you'll see the returns of inflation, cash, bonds (domestic and international or short, medium or long term), stocks (domestic and international, or small, medium and large cap).

Once you've conducted your research and perhaps taken those online surveys to assess your risk appetite, you are now ready to determine your asset allocation. Let's say you determine that 80% stocks and 20% bonds is how you're comfortable being allocated. You then need to determine what investments to construct that allocation. Let's assume you choose index funds.

Index funds are mutual funds or exchange traded funds that track a large or specific aspect of the market. What are some positives of index funds? They are normally very inexpensive, they are broadly diversified, they don't require a lot (normally) to invest initially or on a recurring basis. They are emotionless, and you know what you're getting. A lot of investment companies offer large swaths of index funds. Your research must include which company or companies to use and which of their funds to use.

A very basic structure could be to find funds that broadly track the U.S. stock market, international (non-U.S.) stock markets, U.S. bond market, and international (non-U.S. bond markets). Then you can use these four possible funds to develop a portfolio. Broadly speaking using the above 80% stock and 20% bonds you would invest in the funds you have chosen so your allocation equals 80% stocks and 20% bonds with your initial investment and your on-going investments. Pretty simple huh? A little, but not the whole story. You still need to determine where exactly to invest and the percentage of U.S. versus international (for both stocks and bonds). Then you put it on cruise control.

Those that tout asset allocation would also remind you to rebalance periodically over time. Many say about every year is a good rule of thumb. If you're an 80% stock and 20% bond portfolio holder, over time that percentage would fluctuate. Rebalancing means you simply tweak the percentage in stocks and bonds accordingly. You would sell those that are over the allocation and using those proceeds buy those that are under the allocation. Repeat this year in and year out.

Am I espousing a buy and hold or what is known as a passive investing strategy? It appears that way above. There are many people and firms very comfortable with being more active in their investing strategy. That does not work for a lot of other people. After you've done some solid research online you will see a buy-and-hold strategy (assuming you have broadly diversified, inexpensive index funds, in financially stable investment firms), will do just fine over a long term. No plan, investment, style, allocation, etc. etc. etc. will eliminate all risk. Investing has risk including but not limited to the potential loss of principal. But your research will show that you will do fine over the long term in the passive investing realm.

Then why don't more people do it? Because they get emotional. They think they're smarter than the market. They talked to a friend who told them what to do. They heard online that lots of people are doing "x" or "y." They have FOMO. Or simply put, they get emotional. If you looked at the return percentage of one of the most famous and tracked stock indexes that focuses on large U.S. based companies, you would put your money there and never touch it. This data exists forever and yet people still touch and play with their portfolios, normally to the detriment of their account balances.

Keys are to determine your risk appetite. Determine your asset allocation (the percentage in stock funds and the percentage in bond funds). Research the funds that you feel comfortable using to construct your portfolio for that asset allocation. Rebalance annually and don't touch it. Investing has risk including but not limited to the potential loss of principal regardless of allocation, strategy, style, diversification, etc. etc. etc.

Keep Costs as Low as Possible

Investing has gotten less and less expensive for the average investor over the last handful of decades. Conversely there are still lots of places that are more than happy to take your money and invest for you that are pretty expensive. You must be comfortable doing it on your own, or with the help of a trusted professional that guides you, even if you have the final decision. If you aren't you can pay someone to do it for you.

Every dollar you pay in a fee or expense is taken from your bottom line. If you believe the entire investing landscape is pretty efficient...some do, some don't...meaning all the publicly available information is known and conversely seen in the market price of an investment…then you would make the leap that you as an average investor cannot outsmart the market over the long term. If you've made that leap, (I have), then you would realize that all things being equal, why would you pay more for something if you don't have to? You wouldn't of course.

Again, I do know there a many people that are very active investors that feel comfortable doing more than buy and hold. I am speaking to the average investor who does not want to devote the time, trial and error, expense, etc. to try and generate an above average return. If you actually see what the long-term average returns for a broadly diversified stock and bond index fund would be, you would take that any day of the week…but you MUST buy and hold it.

Here is a very basic example on what costs can do to a return on an investment. My example does not take into account timing, taxes, inflation, actual investing returns, compounding or any of the other things that affect a portfolio – I use simple math. Let's say you decide to go with a professional and their firm charges you 1% per annum based on the principal. If you have a $100,000 account, that 1% would be a $1,000 fee. In another example you chose to use a 0.02% index fund (they exist and many are lower) and have that same $100,000, your annual expense would be $20. Are you kidding me? Nope. What about over 10 years? That would be $10,000 versus $200 respectively. What about 30 years? That would be $30,000 versus $600 respectively. That is money out of your pocket. What happens when your retirement account for example is over a million dollars in the future? Many are. The cost comparison becomes real money.

This example, expenses for having a fund, account or portfolio, does not take into account moving your money in and out of the account of other investments or in and out of other investment companies which many people do all the time. Why? They get emotional.

To truly put this into practice, this and all the principles you must commit (more on this in a little bit) to picking the company you want to use, picking the index fund you want to use, staying balanced and never touching it. You will see a huge impact, especially over 10, 20, 30 years or more. Here is an interesting factoid. When investing in real investments, all of their expenses are publicly acknowledged and reported. If you can't find what an investment costs or what a firm will charge you, feel free to run away or at least not use them as an option.

Costs matter and they may not be discernible with small accounts and over short periods, but they are very impactful over decades of investing. Keep costs as low as possible.

Be Disciplined Over the Long Term

Many of you may know this already and even attempt to follow it. Some of you may disagree with it and that's fine. Many of you have also specifically heard of developing a strong and flexible investment plan using a balanced asset allocation of broadly diversified funds and keeping costs as low as possible. But what makes it all work? Following the plan and being disciplined about it over the long term. Ironically not everyone who knows this and believes it still follows it. That is a key. You may have the best plan on the planet for your goal and your situation, but if you don't follow it, it doesn't amount to a hill of beans.

If there are any changes to your situation, objective, constraints, goals, etc., then it's logical your plan would change. That's why we want to be very methodical on developing a plan to eliminate as many of the reasons people use to change their plan as possible. Even if we take into account every possible circumstance or outcome, plans need to change. That's fine. Establish a new one with all the aforementioned principles and stick to it. Your plan must be flexible enough to withstand life and markets and everything else as much as possible.

Being disciplined over the long term simply means you follow your plan. For example, if your goal of funding for retirement includes a plan of investing 15% of your pre-tax income in your employer's 401k, then you invest 15% of your pre-tax income in your employer's 401k, no matter what. You don't do it when you are fat with cash. You do it every pay period, no matter what.

Being disciplined over the long term simply means when you are investing in your child's college funding plan, you invest every month regardless if the market is up or down, no matter what.

Being disciplined over the long term simply means that when all of your friends are touting the greatness of a new investment or social media is piling on the positives of this investment or that investment, you stick to YOUR plan, no matter what.

Being disciplined over the long term simply means that even if the market tanks 25%, 35% or 45% you stick with it. You don't jump out with the intention of jumping back in when you think it's bottomed out.

There are stats galore online that show many people get out and get in at the wrong times. Again, you assume you're smarter than the market and most people have proven they are not. What has been proven is if you stick to a solid investment plan and don't willy nilly get in and out of investments, it will come back. Yes, it's chaotic if the market tanks around the time you were planning on retirement but sticking to the plan over the long term is normally more positive than trying to time your market moves. Online research will show this. Again, I am talking to the average investor.

Discipline is not hitting the snooze button when your alarm clock goes off. Discipline is working out every day because you know it's good for you. Discipline is maintaining a healthy lifestyle and nutrition regimen. Discipline is living within a budget. Being disciplined over the long term when it comes to your investment plan is the same thing – adhering to those daily, weekly, monthly, and annual behaviors that make your financial plans work. And not succumbing to emotion or the whims of others or the market. It's sticking to the plan, no matter what.

To summarize, the principles of investing include:

1. Develop an Investment Plan Based on Goals
2. Create an Appropriately Balanced Portfolio
3. Keep Costs as Low as Possible
4. Be Disciplined Over the Long Term

Tony brims a little with pride and tells himself, "That's a solid first draft, I'll clean it up tomorrow." He makes a note to call the college tomorrow to coordinate some details but feels good he has what they're looking for.

Retirement Planning

The following day, Tony arrived home from work and said "hey," to Michelle and Isabelle on his way to his office. He put his bag in his office then went and changed into some casual clothes. Michelle had started cooking dinner and Isabelle was sitting at the kitchen island talking with her Mom.

"How was work, Dad?" Isabelle asks.

"It was great!" Tony answers a little too amped.

"What did you do?" Isabelle continues.

"A lot of things, but one thing I got to do was talk with some teammates about funding their retirement plans." Tony seemed excited.

"Can you speak like you're speaking to a fifth grader?" Michelle comments sarcastically nodding toward Isabelle.

"When I say funding retirement, what I really mean are those steps and plans you take to be able to retire, and enjoy the rest of your life without having to work." Tony says ensuring Isabelle is following him. "There are virtually an endless number of financial goals that people may have. We talked about quite of few of them over the past many days. But most people have saving for retirement as a goal. This is an area that a lot of people need help with and should get started earlier than the average person actually does."

"Why is that!?" Isabelle interrupts her Dad.

"Since most everyone has a retirement funding goal, and it's so far off, many people procrastinate and don't get started as early as they should. And because they don't start early, they find they have to make sacrifices later in life to make ends meet. Another thing some people don't realize is the earlier you start the more you'll be able to save since it's so far away. And another thing to remember is a lot of people are living longer than in the past and need to be saving more money for a longer period to ensure they don't run out of money when they are in retirement." Tony looks quizzically at Isabelle hoping she's following along.

Tony continues, "Retirement planning involves

all those steps individuals, couples and families take to comfortably get to the point where they don't have to work full-time, and in theory enjoy the rest of their life. These steps apply to the vast majority of Americans although there are many because of their wealth and affluence do not have to worry about money in a future without work."

"But we do, right?" Isabelle asks.

"We don't worry about it per se," Michelle offers. "But we've been on a journey so we can comfortably stop working when we know it's time."

"That's what planning does." Tony interjects. "It should take the worry out of retirement planning, or any financial goal for that matter."

At that moment Danielle comes into the room and asks, "What's for dinner?"

"Excuse me, we were talking." Michelle says more sternly than necessary.

"Talking about what?" Danielle joins the conversation.

"Mom and Dad are going to retire soon." Isabelle offers some insights.

"That's not exactly what we said," Tony takes the ball. "We are talking about planning financially for retirement so we can retire comfortably when we want to." Tony looks around for understanding.

"I got something in the mail the other day about a pension or something from work." Danielle remembers. "Is that something I need to worry about?" She answers almost dismissively.

Michelle and Tony share a quick, "that's 'your' daughter" look between them.

"I will take a look at it with you later, but yes, that probably pertains to what we're talking about." Tony offers and continues, "Retirement planning can be rather complex but I choose to keep it somewhat simple since our financial situation is not overly complex. I don't want to oversimplify it but want to cover the basics of it with you." Tony states as the ever-present teacher.

"Does it pertain to an I-R-A?" Isabelle blurts out.

"Yes, it does honey, but why are you yelling?" Michelle answers sharing a little smile with Tony.

"That's phenomenal baby doll. IRAs are a part of it. There are some major categories that people need to understand with respect to saving for retirement. They include but are not limited to employer sponsored plans, self-employed plans and individual plans." Tony transitions into full teacher mode. "There are different types of employer plans that operate similarly and some that are quite different. The first one is a pension." Tony looks at Danielle to make the point. "A pension is offered by a lot of government or school type entities and a few commercial companies, and it's a guaranteed income at some point in the future assuming the employee does certain things like works a certain amount of time."

"You have a pension right Dad?" Danielle offers.

"That's right, he has a pension from the military that he earned by serving over 21 years." Michelle answers for Tony while preparing vegetables for a salad.

"Traditional pensions are hugely powerful as they provide a guaranteed income, often for life. However, they have become less and less of an option for employers because they are so expensive to fund and maintain. So, what a lot of employers do now is offer different employer sponsored plans that put the onus on the employee to save for their retirement." Tony checks around the kitchen for understanding.

"You mean like a 401k?" Isabelle offers.

"That's right. How did you know that?" Tony asks as a proud parent.

"I heard you and Mom talking about it the other day." Isabelle offers knowing she hears Mom and Dad talk about a lot of things that are probably not meant for her ears.

"Yes, there are many plans but I will explain what a 401k is. A 401k is a plan that allows the employee to invest monies from their paycheck into an account that holds various investments, mostly index funds, offered by the company that administers the plan. The employee can contribute a certain amount capped by the law. Those monies grow based on the growth of the underlying investments. However, just like any investment plan, investing involves risk and may include but not limited to loss of principal. And there are a lot of tax rules an employee must understand with their contributions, the growth of the account and its use in retirement where they should consult a tax professional or their CPA. In a 401k those monies grow tax-deferred. There are a lot of rules but the basic thing to understand is you can contribute money up to a certain amount and that money grows over time. When you retire you would use that money to fund your retirement. A cool aspect is along with the employee putting money in their 401k, the employer may also add money to the employee's 401k. That's called a match." Tony finishes his thought.

"How much do you do at work, Dad?" Danielle asks keeping up with the lesson.

"I contribute 15% and my employer contributes an additional 8%." Tony answers.

"That's pretty good right?" Danielle says without truly knowing how smart she is.

"That is. Many companies do not offer that liberal of a match. My company does and I take full advantage of it. The rule of thumb is you should maximize your 401k as much as you can but 'NEVER' (Tony uses air quotes) below what the company will match." Tony finishes.

"So, you have a military pension and a 401k from work for your retirement funding?" Isabelle lets everyone know she's following along.

"Yes, but we have a little more." Michelle continues for the team. "I have a pension from a former employer that will kick in when I retire later in life. Your father and I both have Roth and Traditional IRAs, and we both will receive Social Security in the future. And we have other investments and savings accounts that we will use as well." Michelle finishes.

"Wow, we must be rich?" Isabelle asks sheepishly.

"Being rich is relative. We have planned a long time to ensure we won't have to worry about money in retirement. That is not without its sacrifices in our working years. But remember, you have to prepare yourself for not working in the future. When your Mom and I decide to stop working, we don't want to and at our current pace won't have to, worry about being comfortable." Tony says matter of factly.

"Don't I pay in to Social Security?" Danielle asks a question moving in a different direction.

"Everyone who works does. Whether you're self-employed or work for the government or work for a company, you put money into Social Security and the employer does as well. The expectation is the government will then pay you Social Security every month for the rest of your life once you're reached a certain age and started the process." Michelle finishes her thought.

"So, you basically pay into it and then get it all back?" Isabelle asks the $64,000 question.

"Sort of," Tony answers in a noncommittal way. "When Social Security was introduced a long time ago, many Americans had nothing in the form of retirement savings and this offered them some assistance but was never meant to be the sole provider of a person's retirement funds. Sadly, many Americans ONLY (Tony overemphasizes the word) have Social Security in retirement. Your Mom and I will have a Social Security check once we start drawing it in the future. Like everything else in planning for retirement, Social Security has a lot of rules people need to be aware of. But basically, your Mom and I request annual estimated benefits statements from Social Security that tells us what our future benefit might be." Tony offers.

"I heard Social Security won't be around by the time I get to retirement." Danielle asks worriedly.

Michelle and Tony share "the parent look."

"Social Security has changed a lot since its inception and will probably change more in the future. Your father and I believe it will be in our and your future in some form despite all the changes." Michelle finishes.

Tony immediately starts in, "That is a huge reason to not solely rely on Social Security. Many people I know and have worked with don't actually use it in their financial plan, instead treating it as something extra and not relied on. Bottom line, we go online, get our annual estimated benefits statements, and keep plugging along." Tony finishes this portion of his lesson.

"So seriously, what's for dinner?" Danielle asks again getting back to what she finds really important.

"Pasta!!" Michelle ends the discussion about what's for dinner.

"Can you tell us what IRAs are?" Isabelle reminds everyone she was the first to bring it up earlier.

"Along with employer sponsored retirement plans like pensions and 401k's, individual plans include but are not limited to IRAs or Individual Retirement Accounts. They work similar to employer plans but there are notable differences.

All investing involves risk which includes but is not limited to the potential loss of principal. And IRAs involve understanding your tax situation when you contribute and when you start taking distributions that everyone should consult with their tax professional or CPA to ensure they understand everything. An IRA has a maximum amount a person can contribute each year based on the limits set by the law. It also grows tax deferred if certain rules are followed and can be used in the future again if you've followed certain rules. IRAs are very liberal in what you can invest in them and a lot of people stick with mutual funds or ETFs." Tony completes his thought as he grabs a cucumber from Michelle's salad and eats it.

"Do a lot of people invest in all these different places?" Danielle asks a brilliant question.

"Sadly no, but more should. The problems are diverse. Many either don't understand any of it and choose not to, or they perceive they don't have enough money to invest in something so far away, or they feel they will have plenty of time, or worse just don't care." Michelle offers in her motherly tone. "Planning for and investing in your retirement should be a high priority and the earlier you get started the better. Investing now for something 20, 30, 40 or even 50 years away is the true definition of delayed satisfaction." Michelle offers somewhat soberly.

"That's why we budget, right?" Isabelle offers looking to be the teacher's pet.

"That is one hundred percent right, baby doll." Tony answers with a huge smile.

"That's correct honey. When you first start out," Michelle answers and continues while looking straight at Danielle, "getting on and staying on a budget allows you to pay all of your expenses, save, invest, tithe and enjoy yourself, now and the rest of your life. That's why your Dad and I harp on getting on and staying on a budget and remembering to budget for savings and investing early and often." Michelle finishes as she cuts up some tomatoes.

"Man, there's a lot of stuff to know and remember when you plan for retirement." Danielle states.

"It may appear that way now," Tony offers, "but that is one of the reasons I want you two to take personal accountability on reading about and studying the basics of personal finance. People don't just pick it up. They have to work at it. It's one of the most important things you can do. Becoming smart on personal finance is one of the most important things you can do. It sounds cliché but no one gets a second chance to save for retirement. And starting early and investing as much as you can for as long as you can will literally and figuratively pay off in a huge way." Tony completes the lesson.

Michelle finishes up making the salad, looks around the kitchen and unnecessarily announces, "It's time to eat."

Conclusion

Everyone fixed their salad and dinner plates like they've done a thousand times before. The bread, cheese and anti-pasta was on the table. Everyone took their normal seats, and on cue held hands, then Michelle offered a blessing.

That done, everyone started eating. "Dinner is great Momma." Isabelle states the obvious.

"Thanks sweetheart," Michelle says sincerely, "I'm glad someone likes it." Michelle continues in her normal reverse psychology way.

"It's awesome, thanks baby." Tony says between bites.

"We talked about a lot of stuff recently. I am now more confused than before. Where should I start." Danielle asks innocently.

"I think it boils all down to understanding what you want to do financially and when. Then establish specific goals and then the plans to accomplish them. You should commit to slowly but surely doing some personal study about the subject. I also recommend developing a budget that you commit to every day. And along the way your Mom and I (Tony looks at Michelle) will assist every step of the way. This is a lifetime journey, but it all starts with a single step. Please pass me the olives." Tony finishes and switches the subject.

"Amen." Danielle closes for the team.

Key Takeaways

- A widow never told me her husband left her too much life insurance when he died
- Buy low, sell high. If it don't go up, don't buy it. ~ Will Rogers
- Maximize the power of compounding
- A retired couple never told me they saved too much for retirement
- Avoid fads
- If you stay on a budget with 90% of your income (or less) it's really easy to tithe
- Don't make impulsive decisions
- The physical behavior of literally saving and investing every single month your entire working life is one of the most powerful financial tools ever invented
- The stock market goes up over the long term
- Follow your investment plan

- Don't confuse investing brilliance with a bull market
- Diversify, diversify, diversify
- Be appropriately skeptical of so-called "experts"
- When you have consumer debt, commit to paying off the lowest balance first, then the next lowest, then the next lowest, until they're all paid off. The psychological power of decreasing the <u>number</u> of loans you have is more powerful than the money you supposedly save paying off the one with the highest interest rate first.
- Minimize investment expenses as much as possible
- Invest a portion of your income every pay period your entire life and you'll be amazed at how wealthy you will become
- Living a healthy life your entire life does wonders for your health expenses
- Live on a budget your entire life and you'll be amazed at what you can afford
- A lot of people are "house poor." Don't spend too much on your house or all the things that go with owning a house.

- Buying your breakfast, lunch, dinner, coffees, or snacks on the economy is way more expensive than preparing them at home. Remember that when you may live an average of 80 years.

- You won't magically get smarter on the subject of personal finance as you get older. Commit to doing some reading and self-study on the subject

- Has anyone ever said, "Man I got a bad deal at the car dealer?" Everyone says the opposite. How do car dealerships stay in business then?

- If you didn't need it, was getting something on sale a good deal?

- No one gets a second chance to save for retirement

- Go online at least annually and request an estimated benefits statement from the Social Security Administration

- Take advantage of every dollar your employer will match in your employer plan

- Do you know what your risk appetite is? Go online and search for a risk assessment, you may be surprised at how much risk you are willing or not willing to accept.

- Imagine if you invested all of your retirement in a broadly diversified, U.S. stock market index and then literally ignored it for 30 years? Google it. You'll thank me later.
- I could argue your most valuable asset is not your house like a lot of people falsely believe. Your most valuable asset is your ability to earn income
- The financial behaviors (good and bad) of parents, are what their children see and emulate later in life
- Teach your children early and often the value of saving and model it